AMERICAN HORTICULTURAL SOCIETY
PRACTICAL GUIDES

WALLS & FENCES

D1446225

AMERICAN HORTICULTURAL SOCIETY
PRACTICAL GUIDES

WALLS &
FENCES

LINDEN HAWTHORNE

DORLING KINDERSLEY PUBLISHING, INC.
www.dk.com

DORLING KINDERSLEY PUBLISHING, INC.
www.dk.com

PROJECT EDITOR Irene Lyford
ART EDITOR Murdo Culver

SERIES EDITOR Gillian Roberts
SERIES ART EDITOR Stephen Josland
US EDITOR Ray Rogers

SENIOR MANAGING EDITOR Mary-Clare Jerram
MANAGING ART EDITOR Lee Griffiths

DTP DESIGNER Louise Paddick

PRODUCTION Mandy Inness

First American Edition, 2000
2 4 6 8 10 9 7 5 3 1

Published in the United States by
Dorling Kindersley Publishing, Inc., 95 Madison Avenue, New York, NY 10016

Dorling Kindersley Publishing, Inc. offers special discounts for bulk purchases for sales
promotions or premiums. Specific, large-quantity needs can be met with special editions,
including personalized covers, excerpts of existing guides, and corporate imprints.
For more information, contact Special Markets Department, Dorling Kindersley
Publishing, Inc., 95 Madison Avenue, New York, NY 10016 Fax: 800-600-9098

Library of Congress Cataloging-in-Publication Data

Walls & fences. -- 1st American ed.
p. cm. -- (AHS practical guides)
Includes index.
ISBN 0-7894-5071-2 (pbk. : alk. paper)
1. Fences--Design and construction. 2. Brick walls--Design and
construction. 3. Stone walls--Design and construction. I. Series.
TH4965. W35 2000
690'.89--dc21   99-41065
                                          CIP

Reproduced by Colourscan, Singapore
Printed and bound by Star Standard Industries, Singapore

CONTENTS

WALLS AND FENCES FOR YOUR YARD 7

Practical and decorative uses, including security, privacy,
wind protection, changing levels, dividing space, and
screening; fence and wall types and materials, including
decorative elements; legal and safety aspects; planting by
walls and fences.

PRACTICAL PROJECTS 31

GETTING DOWN TO BASICS 58

Walling and fencing materials and posts; cutting bricks;
cement mixes; tools; renting equipment; electrical safety
outdoors; estimating quantities and ordering materials;
glossary of useful terms; building regulations; safety
precautions; site preparation and foundations;
maintenance and renovation.

WALLS AND FENCES FOR YOUR YARD

WHY HAVE WALLS AND FENCES?

WALLS AND FENCES are so commonplace that they are all too easily relegated to the category of "serviceable necessities" as they perform their invaluable role of enclosing your yard and areas within it. To regard these structures as purely utilitarian, however, greatly underestimates their contribution to the overall look of your yard: with just a little imagination, walls and fences can enhance a garden's design in ways that can be as stylish as they are practical.

PRACTICAL OR DECORATIVE USE?

In a crowded world, the natural desire for privacy is frequently uppermost in the minds of homeowners. This is especially true of a garden, which so often provides a retreat from the hurly-burly of modern life. At a basic level, walls and fences fulfill this need in a practical way as well as providing security, shelter, and a means of dividing a site. But practical uses need not exclude decorative appeal: the range of attractive materials and styles available is so diverse that making a suitable choice can seem positively bewildering. A simple listing of your priorities, which takes into account factors such as cost, durability, and style, will help make sure that you get it right first time.

PAINTED WALL
Reflecting light and maximizing radiated warmth, this white-painted, high brick wall alleviates the potential gloom of a shady, private courtyard to the advantage of both gardener and the plants growing at the wall's base. The wall will require repainting from time to time if its benefits are to be maintained.

◀ PICKET FENCE *A white picket fence sets off a cottagey combination of columbines and foxgloves.*

PRACTICAL USES

THE DECISION TO BUILD A NEW WALL OR FENCE is often made primarily for practical reasons – for example to mark a boundary or to screen your yard from the neighborhood. Whatever the main purpose, however, the form and strength of the structure, and the construction methods used, must be capable of withstanding the demands made upon it, bearing in mind that some materials and methods are better suited to specific uses than others.

SECURITY AND PRIVACY

A well-built, high brick or stone wall that is impervious to prying eyes includes among its many advantages the highest possible value in terms of good looks, privacy, and security. You need to consider its position carefully, however, (and more so in some neighborhoods than others) so that in gaining a deterrent to intruders you do not, at the same time, inadvertently provide them with safe cover.

While the initial outlay on materials and labor for a brick or stone wall can be great, long-term maintenance costs are satisfyingly low, and you may even find that it adds to the value of the property.

Where the big outlay on a high wall is out of the question, there are many forms of attractive wooden fencing that will do the job just as adequately. Wooden fences are not only less expensive in materials, they are also far less demanding in terms of specialized building skills and offer great savings in labor costs, since the building and installation of most can be undertaken with a minimum of expertise.

PROVIDING WIND PROTECTION

Creating shelter from strong winds can make a garden more comfortable for people and plants alike, but, although a high wall may seem ideal for this purpose, it does have one major disadvantage: such a solid barrier often creates vortices in its lee,

ON THE DIAGONAL
Although providing less privacy than a wall or closeboarded panels, this wooden fence offers a semi-open method of screening that is particularly useful in windy situations. A dynamic decorative effect is achieved by attaching the boards diagonally across the panels, which are then painted a soft, harmonizing green.

especially in exposed areas. In such cases, consider a semipermeable structure, such as a sturdy trellis fence. Such a wind filter provides shelter by reducing wind speed – an effect that is enhanced by clothing the fence in climbing plants (*see pp.28–29*).

> Terraced walls transform a difficult site into a new planting opportunity

CHANGING LEVELS

On sloping sites, the use of retaining walls to create terraces provides an interesting way of changing levels while transforming difficult conditions into new planting opportunities. On a flat site, raised beds lend the opportunity of introducing height to a design. Their excellent drainage can prove an ideal solution in gardens with poorly drained soils, and they have the added advantage of bringing plants closer to eye level and to a comfortable working height for gardeners of restricted mobility.

▲ BLUE LATTICEWORK
A latticework effect is achieved in this blue-painted fence of narrow, diagonal trellis panels. The open style provides a form of screening that reduces the impact of windflow.

▼ EASY-REACH RAISED BED
A raised bed of reconstituted stone with brick coping brings this planting design to a comfortable working height and enables the plants to be enjoyed at closer quarters.

DECORATIVE USES

A N OLD GARDENING MAXIM directs the designer always to combine use with beauty, and few garden structures offer such great opportunities to put this advice into practice as walls and fences. So great is the wealth of materials available – whether traditional or modern, bought or reclaimed – that walls and fences can be constructed to enhance and decorate your property in stylish and individual ways that are as beautiful as they are functional.

CREATE A BACKDROP

The sheltering warmth and subtle color tones of a mellow brick or aged stone wall have long been appreciated as a visually pleasing backdrop to a planting design. Not only do they lend valuable height to a design, but they also form the ideal background for displaying climbing plants to perfection. Because they absorb the sun's heat by day and release it by night, walls offer a bit of protection to marginally hardy plants that would otherwise grow poorly or die if they were grown in the open garden.

A wooden fence can play a similar role, whether it is allowed to mellow naturally or is stained or painted with modern wood

treatments. The latter are available in a range of colors from the subtle and natural to bright and vibrant finishes.

MYSTERY AND ENTICEMENT

Few of us can resist the invitation, when offered, to explore an area that is merely glimpsed through a gate or archway set into a wall. With imagination, walls and fences lend infinite possibilities for adding an element of irresistible mystery to a design, screening off one area from another

VIBRANT SHAPES AND COLORS
A harlequin effect is achieved in this blue-stained backdrop of pointed pickets, from which diamond shapes have been cut.

▲ PEEPSHOW
A circular peephole, built into a high brick wall, offers an enticing glimpse into the garden beyond.

◀ SERPENTINE WALL
A gently curved wall creates sheltered bays within the border for surpise displays of choice or favorite plants.

so that all is not viewed at once. Try the architects' trick of fenestration – including "peepholes" or *clair voyées* – to frame a view or allow tantalizing glimpses, or simply employ a see-through structure, such as a trellis, to give an enticing hint of what lies beyond.

The serpentine or "crinkle-crankle" wall, which was used in old gardens to create warm bays to ripen fruit, lends itself to

Peepholes offer tantalizing glimpses of the view beyond

reinterpretations for smaller gardens. Use the hidden bays as frames for favorite plants and to add an element of surprise with a succession of cameo plantings.

SPACE DIVIDERS AND SCREENS

Many of the grandest gardens in history use walls and fences as interior dividers of space within the garden. It is a sound principle, even in spaces of more modest scale. Walls or fences can be used to create enclosed garden spaces to suit different activities – for example, to separate the vigorous games-players from the dedicated gardeners of the household, or to separate areas for growing edible crops from more ornamental plantings. They might be used to enclose sheltered areas from the rest of your yard, creating an area for quiet and restful contemplation, or to screen from view unsightly features that lie beyond your property boundaries.

In terms of dividing space within an area, walls and fences play a vital role in creating garden "rooms" for planting designs of different feel and style and are invaluable in remolding difficult shapes, such as a long, narrow area, into more pleasing proportions.

Last, but by no means least, walls and fences are indispensable for disguising those mundane, necessary, but esthetically unappealing items – trash cans, compost piles, and tool sheds – that are inevitable inclusions in most properties.

FENCING TYPES AND MATERIALS

W HETHER IT IS PRIVACY, SECURITY, or simply a boundary marker that you need, there is a type of fencing to fit the bill. At one time, only a restricted palette of brown was on offer, but modern wood treatments have introduced a wealth of colors to tone or contrast with your planting designs. If you can't find anything you like at the garden center or do-it-yourself store, you can adapt the techniques to different materials to produce your own, highly individual design statement.

WHY CHOOSE WOODEN FENCING?

In terms of cost and ease of construction, wooden fences win outright in comparison with brick or stone. Since they demand little in the way of specialized building skills, you can confidently do it yourself and make considerable savings on labor costs.

PANEL FENCING

Fencing falls into two broad categories: those made up of prefabricated panels, like much standard fencing, and those made up of smaller units, such as post-and-rail or picket fences – but there are many variations on each of these themes.

Most prefabricated panels are made up of slats of fir, cedar, or pine, in a variety of widths and heights and designs, including horizontal, vertical, and diagonal orientations. Tall and visually opaque, they provide instant privacy and some shelter but lack the necessary structural strength for security purposes. For this, a better

▲ POST-AND-RAIL BOUNDARY
Horizontal rails secured to wooden uprights make a neat and simple boundary fence but offer little in the way of security.

◄ UNOBTRUSIVE CHAIN-LINK
Plastic-coated chain-link fencing provides a secure barrier that blends into the background when clothed with climbing plants.

▲ SITE DIVIDER
A low panel fence is ideal for dividing a yard into different areas and creates an effective barrier to small animals.

◄ WIND-FILTERING LATTICE
Woven panels provide wind-filtering shelter and a modicum of privacy but lack the structural strength needed for security.

choice is closeboard fencing (*see pp.36–41*), made from overlapping boards or boards joined along their sides. Both can be built from scratch or from prefabricated panels.

LOW AND OPEN FENCING

In yards that simply need a boundary fence, or in areas with legal restrictions on fence heights, post-and-rail, post-and-chain, or picket-style fencing are relatively inexpensive options. These offer little privacy or security, and the more open the

> Remember, the more open the fence, the less security it will offer

structure, the less suitable it is for keeping the neighbor's dog out of your yard. If the last is high on your wish list, consider a low panel or closeboard fence. Where appearance is less important, a chain-link fence forms a very effective barrier and can be camouflaged by growing a vigorous climber through it.

▲ SECURITY AND PRIVACY
A closeboard fence provides security and privacy, while the pale green finish forms a subtle background to a planting design.

SELECTING A STYLE

Style is partly a matter of personal taste, but the most pleasing results are generally achieved by erecting a fence suited to both setting and purpose. Compare the different moods of an informal rural property, set amidst rolling countryside, and the neat plot of a suburban yard or a formally minimalist urban courtyard. The first may

> For the most pleasing results, select a style suited to the setting

require a stockproof, ranchland-style fence that permits unrestricted views of the countryside beyond, but the priority in a suburban plot might be the peep-proof privacy of close-woven panel fencing. In an urban setting, where the strong, geometric lines of nearby buildings dictate a more formal mood, the smooth-planed verticals of a closeboard fence will dovetail perfectly with the surroundings.

▲ RUSTIC CHARM
A fence made of rustic poles provides privacy in a semirural setting while allowing gentle breezes to filter through to the quiet patio area.

▶ RECLAMATION
Old railroad ties can be used to build a sturdy, ecologically friendly fence that is particularly suited to large country spaces. Their well-weathered appearance allows them to look instantly at home.

Picket fences, with all their variations of height and pattern, are among the most versatile of fences, good for both rural and suburban plots. But whereas a rough-hewn picket fence provides the perfect frame for an informal cottage garden, its urban counterpart may be better made of neatly planed lumber painted a clean, crisp white. It is worth bearing in mind the powerful mood-enhancing qualities of color: bright blues and zingy violets may lift the spirits in a modern urban setting, but more pastoral plots almost beg the use of softer sage grays and holly greens.

RECLAIMED MATERIALS

Recycling materials makes sound economic and ecological sense, and architectural salvage centers offer a rich source of unique materials. The mellow, weathered appearance of reclaimed wood has the advantage of looking as if it has been in place forever, but you do need to choose materials with care. While a chunky, rough wooden fence looks perfectly at home in a rural area, and a silver-toned fence made of driftwood forms a perfect frame in a seaside setting, both would look out of place on a modern housing subdivision.

▲ COTTAGE GARDEN SIMPLICITY
A post-and-rail fence, constructed from mellowed rustic poles, blends easily with a relaxed, cottage-garden-style planting of columbines and geraniums.

▼ TEMPORARY MEASURES
Prefabricated rustic snow fencing makes a cheap and instant temporary fence while awaiting full foliage cover from plantings.

VARIATIONS ON A THEME

Observing how gardeners use fencing materials in other parts of the world can be a rich source of inspiration. Think of Japanese gardens, for example, where the soft, neutral colors of bamboo screens form an elegant backdrop to the vertical lines of living bamboos and blend quite naturally with rocks and gravel. You can identify

> Reinforce the overall garden style with fencing detail

and use such stylish elements to lend an Oriental feel to your own designs.

In a similar vein, you might vary the shape of picket-fence pales to pick up and echo decorative detail from the house – for example from an existing porch or ornate wood trim. Fencing detail might reinforce the style of a colonial or Gothic house, or, if you use a more local idiom, harmoniously blend a country house and garden with its surroundings. Such attention to detail lends a valuable element of unity to the overall garden design.

▲ BAMBOO SCREENS
The neutral tones of a bamboo screen provide a perfect backdrop to the rich greens of living plants and add an element of Oriental style.

▼ ORNATE PICKET FENCING
Many variations of picket fencing are possible. Here, the sculpted zigzag top of the fence is echoed in the ornamental shaping of the pales.

▲ OPEN-PATTERN TRELLIS
*This trellis forms a sturdy
screen without restricting
views of surrounding areas.*

◀ CLOSE-PATTERN TRELLIS
*This semisolid barrier lends
wind shelter and privacy as
well as adding an element of
mystery to the view beyond.*

ADAPTING STYLE TO PURPOSE

You may sometimes find that the style of
fence that you've set your heart on does
not agree with your other priorities. If,
for instance, you love the idea of trellis
work but also need wind shelter and
privacy, instead of an open-pattern trellis,
consider using a more solidly made, close-
textured trellis (*see above*). Alternatively,
attach a trellis panel to the top of a more
solid structure, such as a closeboard fence.
Other mixed-media techniques include
topping a low stone or brick wall with a
trellis or, as shown here (*right*), a short
picket atop a low wall. This is an
economical way of building a strong
barrier that still allows views in and out.

USING WOOD OUTDOORS

All outdoor wood must be treated with
preservative. Most purchased lumber is
already pressure-treated and subsequently
needs only the occasional treatment to
maintain it. The most common form of
pressure treatments impart a green tinge to
the wood, which is easily disguised with a
special, exterior formula "microporous"

wood paint (for opaque color) or wood
stain (for translucent effects that enhance
the grain). Most also include preservative.
If you prefer a natural wood finish, seek
out special landscape lumber that has been
pressure-treated with clear preservative.
Protect vulnerable end grain (at the cut
ends of boards or posts) with special
coping rails or weather caps (*see p.41*).

▼ ROUGH WOODEN PICKET
*A low slate wall finished with picket fencing
provides a substantial boundary that blends
perfectly into the local landscape.*

WALLING TYPES AND MATERIALS

BOUNDARY WALLS HAVE BEEN USED to demarcate and protect areas since land was first enclosed for cultivation and reached their zenith in the walled gardens of the Victorian era. While such tall, expensive features have largely been replaced by less costly wooden fences, the decorative and practical advantages of smaller walls have been brought well within the scope of the competent homeowner by the wealth of modern materials available and their relative ease of construction.

CHOOSING THE RIGHT MATERIALS

Walling materials fall into three broad groups: stone, brick, and concrete. Each has many variations. Some require high levels of skill to produce a result that will please you throughout a wall's long life, so, if you intend to do it yourself, be realistic in your aspirations and match the ease of construction with your own level of skill. Consider, too, how well the color and texture of your possible choices will blend with your home and its setting and whether they will give the look you have in mind.

STONE WALLS

Natural stone walls are made from dressed, rough-dressed, or undressed stone: all are obtainable from a stone supplier or local quarry. Whether laid dry or jointed with mortar, stone walls are costly but hard to beat if you want an informal wall that blends seamlessly into its environment.

Drystone walls are usually made from rough- or undressed stone. Both demand time and skill in construction: the wall's ultimate strength depends on each stone fitting snugly with its neighbor, like the pieces of a jigsaw. In areas with a tradition of drystone walls, you can often find weekend courses to learn the basics.

DRYSTONE WALL
This drystone wall illustrates how stones of different shapes and sizes are dovetailed to form a wall whose strength does not rely on mortar. Its intricate construction is both highly skilled and time consuming.

Dressed stone is more costly, but it is the easiest of natural materials to use since it is shaped for uniformity. If the high cost is out of the question, however, you might try reconstituted stone. The best is almost indistinguishable from the real thing, and construction is as simple as laying bricks, producing a perfect effect where a formal, uniform finish is wanted.

KIT-FORM STONE WALLS

If ease of construction is paramount, try a kit form of drystone walling, which gives realistic results with minimal skill.

> It is easy to locate a type of brick to suit your particular setting

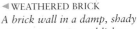

▲ RECONSTITUTED STONE
Preformed blocks of reconstituted stone are simple to put together and much cheaper than quarried stone. Here, they make both a raised bed and a high wall that absorbs traffic noise.

BRICK WALLS

The uniform shape and size of bricks makes construction relatively easy and produces a result that is well suited to formal designs.

The color, finish, and durability of a brick wall is dictated by the type of clay and processes used in the manufacture of the bricks. Clay color shows considerable local variation, and it is easy to locate a type to suit your local setting. Bricks are rated according to strength and weather resistance, so it is important to check that your choice is suitable for the job in hand.

Brick walls must be finished with coping to prevent water penetration from above and the damage that would be caused by subsequent freezing and thawing.

◄ WEATHERED BRICK
A brick wall in a damp, shady site attracts moss and lichen and will weather attractively.

▼ PROTECTIVE COPING
Coping prevents rain from seeping into the wall; a stone sphere adds a grand touch.

▲ FOUNTAIN NICHE
Adding the vitality of moving water to the design – and benefiting the irises growing below – a sandstone Neptune water spout is built into a niche in this drystone wall.

▼ BOLDLY MODERN
A blue-painted stuccoed wall, topped by a picket fence of the same color, makes a strikingly modern backdrop to the plants in this courtyard garden.

HARMONIZING DETAILS

The construction of brick and stone walls provides an opportunity to incorporate design details that will dovetail them firmly into their setting, whether this be in choice of materials and style or as an echo of vernacular architecture.

Stone does this in an obvious way. For example, if the native bedrock consists of sandstone, then walls made of the same materials will blend naturally into the landscape. You might also want to include one of the many regional variations in coping or capping styles.

The bonding patterns of brickwork (*see p.52*), although often used simply for their structural strength or decorative quality, may also be chosen because they reflect either the building tradition in an area or an historical architectural period.

VERSATILE CONCRETE

Concrete has an unfortunate utilitarian image – due, perhaps, to its immense strength and widespread use in industry. Nevertheless, with just a little imagination, concrete can be one of the most practical and versatile of walling materials.

Concrete blocks are among the cheapest of hard materials, and their uniformity and relatively large unit size make for quick and

STUCCO AND APPLIED SHELL ART
A stylized pattern, created with mussel and cockle shells, has been applied to the terracotta-colored stucco on this stone wall. A variegated ivy creeps up to join the blue flower motif.

simple construction. Disguising their appearance can be achieved in a variety of ways: the most common is to use a veneer of beautifully finished facing bricks, which reduces the cost in comparison with an all-brick wall without compromising structural strength. Dressed stone can be used in a similar way. When finished with a brick or stone capping, a concrete wall is almost indistinguishable from the real thing.

> Alcoves provide a frame for focal features such as statuary and fountains

Perhaps the most versatile disguise is a stucco veneer. This mixture of masonry cement and fine sand can be patterned by scoring, brushing, or imprinting, or adorned with applied decoration. Stucco can also be painted with exterior masonry paint. White or honey tones lend a Mediterranean touch to a design, while brighter colors can transform a dingy urban yard into a vibrant, thoroughly modern design feature. Do check, however, that the colors you choose comply with local ordinances and building codes.

FOCAL FEATURES

Walls constructed of brick, stone, or concrete are infinitely more versatile than wooden constructions when it comes to incorporating alcoves designed to frame focal features such as a piece of statuary, a water fountain, or a choice specimen plant.

Sheltered niches are the ideal location for plants that need a little extra warmth; alcoves also make a perfect frame for decorative fruit-tree forms, such as fans or espaliers, and provide valuable protection during the vulnerable flowering and fruit-setting period.

SECURE ATTACHMENTS

Solid walls provide a secure and durable mounting surface for a fountain spout. The sight and sound of moving water adds a pleasant dimension to a garden design, approaching perfection when the materials blend harmoniously or contrast subtly with each other (*see facing page, above*).

▶ SEASIDE THEME
A fan-shaped insert of scallop shells provides variation in color and texture to the dark-colored stones in a seaside garden's drystone wall.

▼ GLEAMING GLASS
Green glass bottle ends embedded in a brick wall enliven its uniformity by adding both color and an attractive, translucent gleam to the surface.

you might incorporate a fine-textured mosaic of small, smooth pebbles gleaned from beaches over the years.

Such decorative touches can also provide a simple but effective means of emphasizing a garden style: a scallop-shell mosaic (*see above*) or a collection of seaside fossils, for example, could reinforce the theme of a coastal garden.

FOUND MATERIALS

Designs that include found or reclaimed materials are easy on both the eye and the pocket and often carry with them the added satisfaction of creating a unique structure. Pieces of water-worn glass from

APPLIED DECORATION

Perhaps more than any other technique, the application of a decorative finish to a wall's surface provides a means of stamping your own, individual identity on the design. You might, for example, use the opportunity to include elements that represent events in your family history, thus making a highly personal and permanent memento.

Champagne bottle bottoms incorporated into a wall, as shown above, could mark a series of family celebrations while at the same time introducing a translucent gleam to an otherwise functional structure. Or

Create a unique design
by incorporating found
materials into a wall

beach or river bed, shards of pottery found during garden digging, or chunks of mason-worked stone from the architectural salvage merchant can all be used for added decorative interest. Or you could use rough chunks of found rock crystals and glass nuggets, in the time-honored fashion, to create a grotto effect.

Since the most appealing results are usually achieved by restricting intense detail to relatively small areas, you can justify the purchase of costly materials such as brilliantly colored ceramic or tiny mirror tiles; these would be prohibitively expensive if used on a large scale, but you can often find such precious oddments in closeout sales.

This technique is perfect for imparting a Moorish style to your designs – for example by creating miniature mosaic panels set against a lapis blue background, as shown below. If you're really ambitious, you can apply pictorial mosaics in the style of a Romanesque fresco. Almost any durable material can be used, but rough-textured items give the strongest bond.

SUCCESSFUL APPLICATION

Planning ahead is vital to the success of such detailed work, so mark out your design on graph paper before you start, and sort your materials by texture and color. Embed applied materials to at least two-thirds of their depth in a stucco or cement surface: a builder's float is the ideal tool for this and gives a fairly level finish. Work on a small area at a time, so that the cement does not dry before you finish. When the concrete is firm, reveal the final beauty by removing excess concrete with a stiff-bristled brush and a spray of clean water.

▲ MIRROR-TILE MOSAIC
A trompe l'oeil effect of depth and distance is achieved here by the application of a mirror-tile mosaic that reflects the border planting.

▼ MOORISH INFLUENCE
Mosaic detail on the lapis blue ground of a courtyard wall evokes an atmosphere of Mediterranean sun and warmth.

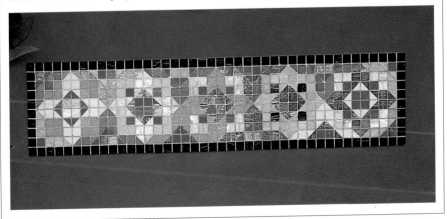

PRACTICAL CONSIDERATIONS

WHETHER THE INTENDED PURPOSE of your wall or fence is simply a boundary marker or to provide a more substantial or decorative structure, you will have thought through the suitability, desirability, and cost of the proposed materials and design. But before ordering materials and beginning the physical labor of building your wall or fence, there are a number of factors to be considered to ensure that your project is legal, safe, and easily manageable.

LEGAL ASPECTS

In rural areas, there are generally no legal restrictions regulating the style and dimensions of walls and fences on private property. However, in many urban and suburban areas there are codes and ordinances on the books that must be met if you want to construct anything on the property. It is up to the homeowner to contact local government officials to find out what the building codes entail and if there are any fees that must be paid. Contractors may also need to be involved in this process.

Common factors regulated by building codes include the height of a structure and the minimum distance it can begin from the street, sidewalk, public easement, utility pole, neighbor's house or property, or other adjacent area. In some municipalities the "better" side of a fence must face toward your neighbor or the street, with the less attractive side toward your property.

Make sure your project meets local building codes and ordinances

---

SAFETY CONSIDERATIONS

Building materials are heavy, so when lifting, take due care to hold the weight close to your body, keep your back straight, and let your thigh muscles take the strain (*see p.65*). Wear sturdy shoes and use protective gloves, especially when working with cement and mortar and

FLATTERING FOLIAGE
A high brick wall provides long-lasting, low-maintenance, effective security, but its construction is usually a job for a professional builder. To soften the brash look of new red brick, grow shrubs up and over the wall.

INNATE CHARM
With dense planting on the other side creating an effective deterrent barrier, it hardly matters that this tumbledown, rustic picket fence provides little in the way of security: its immense visual charm more than makes up for the lack of functional strength.

handling rough stones and brick. If you are cutting brick or stone, protect your eyes with goggles, and, when using electrical tools outdoors, ensure that they are properly grounded.

STRUCTURAL SAFETY

Walls need firm foundations to support and distribute their weight; their depth depends on the size of wall (*see p.66*). A single-course wall (half a brick thick) should be no higher than 28in (70cm); anything taller requires a double course. As a rule, walls higher than 3ft (1m) need the additional strength of built-in piers. The greater level of technical skills demanded by higher walls is beyond the scope of most amateurs; in this case, call in the professionals.

CHOOSING A PROFESSIONAL

Personal recommendation may be the simplest route to finding a reliable builder. Failing that, the local garden center or builder's supply store may have contacts.

When you've made a short list, ask to see samples of completed work, obtain and compare competitive estimates, and check whether insurance-backed guarantees are offered. The latter ensures that any failure is the builder's responsibility, not yours. Finally, draw up a written contract stating the nature of the work, proposed timescale, and terms of payment.

BE PREPARED

- Building materials are both heavy and high volume: wherever possible, arrange delivery directly to the site and recruit a team of willing helpers to help shift materials.
- Bricks and cement must be kept dry, so have a wooden pallet ready to keep them off the ground and cover them with watertight plastic or a tarpaulin until required.
- If you live in a townhouse and need to carry materials through the house, take steps to protect interior walls and surfaces.
- Building work is hard, physical labor so, if you're unused to exercise, warm up first to reduce the risk of strains or sprains.

PLANTING BY WALLS AND FENCES

S O DIVERSE ARE THE NEW PLANTING SITES created by the introduction of a wall or fence into the garden that an avid gardener may build one just to take advantage of these opportunities. To maximize the use of such structures, however, and to make the most successful choice of plants that will flourish in the conditions created, a little forethought and some understanding of the ways in which walls and fences influence the surrounding microclimates are required.

SUN, SHADE, AND RAIN SHADOW

If you look at the base of a wall just after a shower, you will see clearly the effects of rain shadow. In an area up to 18in (45cm) from the base, the soil will be drier than that which lies just beyond. This is why wall-trained shrubs and climbers, which need moisture for good growth, should be planted at least 18in (45cm) away from the wall's base. But this doesn't mean that rain-shadow areas are unsuitable for planting: they are, in fact, the perfect site for bulbs (such as nerines or *Amaryllis belladonna*) that require hot, dry summers for good flowering.

The reflected warmth from the sunniest walls often creates local hot spots. Some plants, such as astilbes or primulas, find such sites unendurable, but there are many plants that thrive in the heat. Gray-leaved plants – like santolinas, salvias, and some artemisias – or Mediterranean natives, such as rosemary and rock roses (*Helianthemum*) are perfectly adapted to these conditions and often justify their inclusion by flowering more freely here.

Every sunny wall has its shady side, but shade is not a problem: it's an opportunity to increase the range of plants you grow. In damp shade, shade-lovers produce lush growth, retain their color, and remain in peak condition for longer periods. Some will even tolerate dry shade: choose these for the rain-shadowed base of a shady wall.

▲ HOT, DRY AREA
Soil in the lee of a sunny wall is hot and sheltered from rain, requiring extra care in the choice and maintenance of plants.

▲ SPEEDY COVERAGE
*Golden hops (*Humulus lupulus 'Aureus'*) will rapidly cover an unsightly wall or fence with its bright yellow foliage.*

SHADY AREA
A high brick wall blocks out light in this corner but provides the perfect conditions for shade-tolerant plants. Many of these give a lush display that continues to look good when plants in sunny positions are past their best.

FROST POCKETS

Cold air behaves just like water – it flows downhill and accumulates in the lowest-lying hollows to create what is known as frost pockets. If air flow is unimpeded, the potential cold damage caused to plants is minimized, but a wall or fence at the bottom of slope acts as a barrier to the

> Shade provides an opportunity to grow a wider range of plants

flow and risks creating a frost pocket. This likelihood is reduced if permeable fences such as picket are used, but it is sometimes unavoidable. Do not despair: cold areas are not "no-go" areas for planting. Simply choose plants from the many that are reliably hardy; also consider plants that don't emerge until late in spring when danger of severe frosts has passed.

SUITABLE PLANTS

HOT SPOTS

Crinum × powellii Fragrant, funnel-shaped, showy pink flowers in late summer.
Phlomis italica Gray-leaved subshrub with pink flower spikes in summer.
Rosmarinus officinalis (**Rosemary**) Aromatic evergreen shrub with blue flowers in spring.
Salvia officinalis (**Sage**) Aromatic gray foliage and spikes of blue flowers in summer.
Stachys byzantina (**Lamb's tongue**) Silver-gray leaves and woolly flower spikes in summer.

DRY SHADE

Alchemilla mollis Lime green foliage and sprays of tiny yellow flowers in summer.
Iris foetidissima Seedpods split in autumn to reveal shiny orange-red seeds.
Liriope muscari Evergreen leaves and spikes of tiny purple flowers in autumn.
Symphytum ibericum Robust groundcover with pale yellow flowers in late spring.
Tellima grandiflora Groundcover with long-lived spikes of pale green flowers in summer.
Tolmeia menziesii 'Taff's Gold' Groundcover with gold-and-cream-mottled leaves.

▲ ROCK PLANTS
Crevices in a stone wall
provide ideal conditions
for a variety of rock plants,
including echeveria: drainage
is good and the plants have a
cool root run.

▶ CLIMBERS AND TRAILERS
Walls provide excellent
opportunities for both trailing
and climbing plants. Here,
orange nasturtiums tumble
over the tiered branches of
Cotoneaster horizontalis.

PLANTS FOR RAPID COVER

Although it's often best to train wall plants over several seasons, more rapid cover will be needed if you inherit an unsightly wall or wish to clothe a chainlink fence to form a peep-proof barrier. If you need temporary cover while permanent plantings establish, try quick-growing annuals, such as morning glories (*Ipomoea*) or hyacinth bean (*Lablab*), or perennials, such as the golden-leaved hops (*Humulus lupulus* 'Aureus').

For permanent cover, choose woody-stemmed climbers, but remember that only evergreens will be effective all year round.

SUPPORTING CLIMBERS

Different types of climber require different types of support. Self-clinging climbers, such as English ivy or Boston ivy, have adhesive pads that stick to any surface that offers support, such as masonry, wood, or tree bark. They need initial guidance to a wall or fence, then become self-supporting. Twiners, tendril-climbers, and scramblers, like wisteria, clematis, or winter jasmine (*Jasminum nudiflorum*), need a permanent support such as wires and vine eyes or a trellis. Scramblers will need tying in throughout their life, but twiners and tendril-climbers attach themselves firmly to their support once they are established.

All supports must be strong enough to bear the weight of the mature plant and should be mounted 4–6in (10–15cm) away from the wall to ensure good air circulation and minimize the risk of fungal diseases.

CHOOSING WALL PLANTS

Walls provide the ideal habitat not just for the obvious climbers and wall shrubs but for a whole range of plant groups. A hollow wall can be planted with trailers, such as *Phlox subulata, Aurinia saxatilis,* or even groundcover roses to cascade down the face, while the crevices in a dry-stone wall are ideal for rock plants, especially cushion formers that revel in perfect drainage. Shade lovers will thrive

---

A sunny drystone wall provides perfect niches for many rock plants

---

on the shady side of a wall.

As well as plants that enjoy the added warmth of a wall, the most successful wall shrubs are those with long, flexible stems, such as honeysuckle, those that tolerate clipping to shape, like firethorn, and shrubs with a two-dimensional habit, such as *Cotoneaster horizontalis,* with its fans of horizontally tiered branches.

PLANTS FOR RAPID COVER

ANNUALS AND PERENNIALS

Cobaea scandens Bell-shaped greenish white flowers age to purple in summer to autumn.
Eccremocarpus scaber Tubular yellow-orange flowers from early summer to autumn.
Humulus lupulus 'Aureus' (**Golden hops**) Golden foliage and attractive fruits.
Lathyrus odorata (**Sweet pea**) Scented flowers ranging from pure white through pink and mauve to deep purple in summer.
Tropaeolum peregrinum (**Canary creeper**) Canary-yellow flowers all summer.

WOODY-STEMMED CLIMBERS

Clematis montana Pink or white flowers in spring.
Fallopia baldschuanica Rampant climber with sprays of white flowers in late summer.
Lonicera periclymenum (**Honeysuckle**) Fragrant yellow or white and pink flowers mid- to late summer.
Vitis coignetiae Large sculptural leaves with orange, red, and yellow autumn tints.

SHARED FENCING
A colorful display of herbaceous perennials provides a cheerful view for neighbors on either side of a picket fence. If you wish to grow a climber on a shared boundary such as this, it would be courteous to consult your neighbors first. You might even persuade them to share pruning duties.

BUILDING FENCES

WOODEN FENCES

WOODEN FENCES ARE RELATIVELY QUICK and simple to erect, using readily available materials and demanding little in the way of specialized building skills. They can provide almost instant privacy and wind shelter and are among the structures most commonly used as boundary markers. Equally importantly, fences offer great potential as decorative garden features, whether painted or stained or harmoniously clothed with wall shrubs and climbers.

MAKING A PANEL FENCE

Panel fences are among the easiest of installations: prefabricated panels are simply attached to a series of wooden or concrete uprights. Wooden posts have the esthetic edge, but they are prone to rot and require regular maintenance throughout their life. Concrete posts are grooved, so slotting panels in place is quite easy, both during the initial construction and later, should any damaged panels need replacing.

Concrete post

Fence panel

Gravel board of wood or preformed concrete

Crushed stone base topped with concrete

PRACTICAL HINTS
- For longevity and low maintenance, choose concrete posts and gravel boards.
- Apply a coat of liquid manure to encourage moss growth on stark new concrete.

CONSTRUCTION OF A PANEL FENCE
A prefabricated panel is slotted into concrete posts. The gravel board protects the panel from rot by preventing contact with the soil.

◄ ADDING HEIGHT *A hedge of* Cotoneaster lacteus *increases both privacy and shelter.*

YOU NEED:

TOOLS
- String and pegs
- Measuring tape
- Spade
- Level
- Claw hammer
- Paintbrush

MATERIALS
- Crushed stone and concrete for setting posts in place
- 4in (10cm) square concrete posts
- 2 x 6ft (2m) fence panels
- Preformed concrete gravel boards
- Wooden capping rail
- Wood preservative
- Galvanized nails

ERECTING THE FENCE POSTS

1 Mark out the fence line with string and pegs. Dig a 30in- (75cm-) deep hole and pack a 6in- (15cm-) layer of crushed stone in the base. Set a concrete post in place. Check its height against the panel. Adjust height, adding more stone as necessary.

2 Place a level against the concrete post to check that it is vertical. Pack more crushed stone around the post to hold it in place, then check again that it is vertical.

3 Pour concrete into the hole around the post. Tamp down with a scrap of wood to dispel air bubbles. Keep adding and tamping concrete until it is just below ground level.

POSITIONING THE PANEL AND FINISHING

4 **Lay the panel** on the ground with the base against the string line. Mark the position of the next hole, making allowances for the depth of the grooves in the posts.

5 **Dig a hole** for the second post and fill with a 6in- (15cm-) layer of stone. Slot the gravel board into the groove in the post; adjust the soil level so the board is horizontal.

6 **Fit the panel** into the groove in the first post, above the gravel board. Place the second post in the hole and slot the ends of the gravel board and panel into the groove, adjusting the stone level as necessary. Pack the post into position with stone and fill the hole with concrete as with the first post. Repeat with more panels and posts to the desired length of the fence.

7 **Cut a length** of capping rail to fit the top of each panel and treat the cut ends with wood preservative. Mount the rail to the top of the panel with galvanized nails. The rail protects the end grain of the panel boards by shedding rainwater away from the fence top.

DEALING WITH SLOPES

Fences on sloping ground can either be built as a series of stepped horizontal runs or made to slope with the ground. Because panel fences lose structural strength if cut, they must be stepped. Uprights must be longer than those required on level ground, the extra height depending on the gradient and the width of the panels. The wedge-shaped gap beneath the panel is filled with a gravel board that is shaped to fit (*see below, left*).

Sloping fences are made of boards nailed to rails that run parallel to the slope. The boards sit vertically on the gravel board, with bases angled to match the slope. Use a template to help cut the correct angle.

STEPPED PANEL FENCE
Shaped gravel boards provide a horizontal base for a stepped panel fence. A more weatherproof, although costly, alternative is to build a stepped series of low brick walls between the posts to create a level base.

SLOPING CLOSEBOARD FENCE
With support posts installed vertically in concrete foundations, and cross-rails and gravel board running parallel to the ground, each board is nailed vertically in place, its base angled to match the slope.

LEVELING A SLOPE

With steeper slopes than those shown above, it is advisable to create a level base between the posts for each panel or fence run. For each section, drive in a stake at the top and bottom of the slope. Stretch a string line between the two and find the horizontal with a builder's line level. Excavate the soil to create a level base that is parallel to the line. Repeat the procedure for each section to achieve a stepped series of level bases for the fence.

CROSSWAYS SLOPE

If a slope traverses your garden so that your neighbor's land is higher than your own, a wooden fence will need to be set on a brick retaining wall to protect the fence from rot through contact with soil. Legally, such a wall must lie entirely within your property, but you may need access to your neighbor's land to construct it. Avoid any disputes by consulting courteously before work begins.

ALTERNATIVE METHODS OF SUPPORT

There are methods of installing wooden posts that reduce rot by keeping them clear of wet soil. Metal post supports are excellent in stone-free soils; in stony soils, they may bend on impact and are best set in concrete. Use 24in (60cm) supports for fences up to 4ft (1.2m) high; 30in (75cm) for fences up to 6ft (2m) high. In stony soil, you could also use concrete spurs.

USING METAL POST SUPPORTS

1 **Set the fixing** accessory on a scrap of wood in the post support socket. Drive the post into the ground with a sledgehammer.

2 **Keep checking** with a level that the post support is vertical. Be sure to check the level on all 4 sides of the support.

3 **Insert the fence** post into the socket at the top of the post support. Secure in place by nailing through the slatted holes with galvanized nails.

SET IN CONCRETE

In stony ground, avoid bending or twisting damage to metal post supports by setting them in a concrete foundation so that the bottom of the support socket sits flush with the ground.

Alternatively, use a concrete spur set in a concrete foundation: this will keep both wooden posts and fence panels well clear of damp ground. Spurs are made with predrilled holes for bolting the uprights securely to them. Before erecting, match up, mark, and drill corresponding holes in the wooden posts.

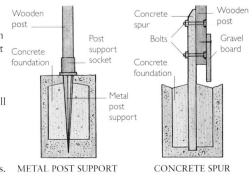

Wooden post
Concrete foundation
Post support socket
Metal post support

METAL POST SUPPORT

Concrete spur
Bolts
Concrete foundation
Wooden post
Gravel board

CONCRETE SPUR

MAKING A CLOSEBOARD FENCE

Closeboard fencing not only offers neat, clean lines that suit both urban and rural settings, it is also one of the strongest forms of fencing and provides almost instant privacy and security.

Prefabricated closeboard panels are available but cannot be satisfactorily cut to size, so custom building is the best and simplest option for awkward spaces.

The fence can be finished with wood stain in natural or vibrant colors, or painted with opaque, exterior-grade microporous wood paints.

PRACTICAL HINTS

• Be sure to provide adequate foundations for uprights: as a general rule, you'll need a 24in- (60cm-) deep hole for fences 4–5ft- (1.2–1.5m-) high, or a 30in- (75cm-) deep hole for a 6ft- (2m-) high fence.
• Always choose pressure-treated lumber for outdoor use. Disguise the characteristic green tint with paint or stain, or seek out landscaping lumber that has been pressure-treated with a clear preservative. Treat newly cut surfaces with wood preservative.
• Use a spacer gauge, cut to the width of one board minus the overlap to ensure that each board uniformly overlaps its neighbor.

YOU NEED:

TOOLS
• Measuring tape
• Saw
• Chisel
• Claw hammer
• Paintbrush
• Spade
• Level
• Screwdriver
• Drill

MATERIALS
• 4in (10cm) square wooden posts
• 6 x 1in (15 x 2.5cm) lumber for gravel board
• 3 x 1in (8 x 2.5cm) lumber for cross-rails
• Wood preservative
• Crushed stone
• Instant concrete mix
• 6 x 1in (15 x 2.5cm) lumber for battens
• Screws
• Galvanized nails
• Feather-edged boards
• Wooden capping rail
• Wooden post caps

PARTS OF A CLOSEBOARD FENCE

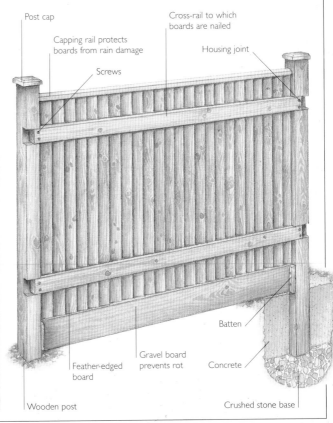

Post cap

Capping rail protects boards from rain damage

Screws

Cross-rail to which boards are nailed

Housing joint

Batten

Feather-edged board

Gravel board prevents rot

Concrete

Wooden post

Crushed stone base

◀ CLOSEBOARD FENCE *A dark stain provides a fine foil for a flowering almond* (Prunus triloba).

PREPARING THE POSTS

1 **Cut the posts** to length: here, 6ft (2m) for a final height of 5ft (1.5m) on 24in- (60cm-) deep foundations. Mark the position for the bottom edge of the gravel board 18in (45cm) from the post base. Rails should sit about 30in (75cm) from the post base and 12in (30cm) below the fence top.

2 **Mark out** on the post the sections to be removed to house the cross-rails. With the post held firmly in a vise, make several saw cuts down to a depth of 1in (2.5cm).

3 **Using a chisel** and hammer, and working away from your body, remove the marked-up lumber section. Paint the cut section with wood preservative. Repeat with each post.

SETTING THE POSTS IN INSTANT CONCRETE

1 **Dig a 24in- (60cm-) hole** and pack with 6in (15cm) of stone. Position the post with cut sections at the back, checking that it is vertical. Fill the hole with dry concrete mix.

2 **Pour water** over the dry concrete mix according to manufacturer's instructions. Before the concrete has set, check that the post is still vertical, repositioning if necessary.

3 Set the second post in the same way, checking that it is vertical and that its position is accurate for the proposed line of the fence.

4 With both posts in place, put the first cross-rail in position; check that it is horizontal. Make any adjustments that may be necessary.

ATTACHING THE GRAVEL BOARD AND CROSS-RAILS

1 Using galvanized nails, attach a wooden batten to the inner surface of the lower part of each post, placing them so that the gravel board will be flush with the posts.

2 With a level, check that the gravel board is horizontal, making any necessary adjustments. Nail the gravel board to the battens, using 2 nails to each batten.

3 Screw the cross-rails into the prepared housing joints in the support posts, positioning them halfway into the cut sections. Use a hand- or electric drill to make guide holes, then screw cross-rails firmly into place.

ATTACHING THE BOARDS

1 **Mark out** and cut the boards to the required fence height, from the top of the gravel board to 3in (8cm) below the post top.

2 **Position the first** board on top of the gravel board and butt it up against the support post. Fit by tapping the board gently into place.

3 **Attach the board** to the top cross-rail with 2 galvanized nails. Check the level, then fit to lower rail.

4 **Lay a spacer gauge** over the first board; position a second board to overlap the first by ½–⅜in (10–12mm).

5 **Nail the board** to the top rail with 1 galvanized nail. Check that it is vertical, then nail to the bottom rail.

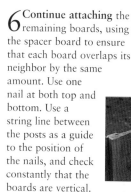

6 **Continue attaching** the remaining boards, using the spacer board to ensure that each board overlaps its neighbor by the same amount. Use one nail at both top and bottom. Use a string line between the posts as a guide to the position of the nails, and check constantly that the boards are vertical.

FINISHING AND WEATHERPROOFING

1 **Measure and cut** the last board to fit the remaining space, with the broadest edge butted up against the post. Nail into position.

2 **Measure and cut** the capping rail to fit between the posts. Carefully nail into place, through the rail, and into the ends of the boards. Nail a wooden post cap to each support post.

VARIATIONS ON THE CLOSEBOARD THEME

Instead of using overlapping, feather-edged boards, a closeboard fence can be made of butt-jointed boards of equal thickness. This produces a fence that is every bit as sturdy but more versatile in terms of varying the height and width of the boards and adding decorative detail. For example, the boards can be cut to different heights to give a castellated effect, or shaped along the top into serpentine curves. Drilled or cut perforations of diamonds, circles, or even quatrefoils add an individual flourish.

BUTT-BOARD FENCE
A simple butt-board fence takes on elegant detail by introducing a variation in height and a simple, Gothic-style motif of drilled trefoil perforations. The horizontally cut board tops are protected by short lengths of capping rail and the whole fence treated with wood preservative.

MAKING A PICKET FENCE

In terms of privacy and security, a picket fence is more decorative than functional, but, nevertheless, it makes an ideal boundary marker and will certainly keep the neighbor's dog out of your yard.

A simple, white-painted picket is the traditional companion for a clapboard or colonial-style house, while its unpainted counterpart – made from rougher lumber – is a perfect frame for the cottage-style garden. Combine the simplicity of construction with the wealth of modern paint and stain finishes available, however, and the

picket fence is versatile enough for even the most contemporary setting. Insert changes by alternating long and short pales, or, instead of round- or pointed-topped pales, use a jigsaw to create more decorative outlines.

PRACTICAL HINTS

- If you intend to paint your picket fence, choose planed timber, which has a smoother surface than rough, unplaned boards.
- Use unplaned boards for a more rustic effect; they are cheaper, too.
- Introduce decorative detail by varying pale heights, or by shaping the tops of support posts and individual pales.

PARTS OF A PICKET FENCE

YOU NEED:

TOOLS
- Measuring tape
- Saw
- Sandpaper
- Straightedge
- Set square
- Claw hammer
- Drill
- Screwdriver
- Post driving tool
- Level
- Paintbrush

MATERIALS
- 3 x 1in (7.5 x 2.5cm) planed lumber for cross-rails and pales
- Galvanized nails
- Screws
- 3in (7.5cm) fence posts
- 3in (7.5cm) spiked metal post supports
- Colored wood stain or exterior wood paint

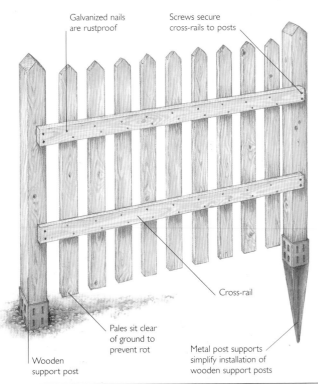

Galvanized nails are rustproof

Screws secure cross-rails to posts

Cross-rail

Pales sit clear of ground to prevent rot

Wooden support post

Metal post supports simplify installation of wooden support posts

◀ ZIGZAG PICKET *Echoing the pointed tops of pales and posts, this fence is cut into a zigzag shape.*

CUTTING THE PALES

1 **Having decided** on the ultimate fence height, cut the planed lumber into pales of the required length.

2 **Make a template** from cardboard for the chosen shape for the top of the pales and mark out each length.

3 **With a saw,** carefully cut the top of the pales to the required shape. Smooth the cut edges with sandpaper.

ATTACHING PALES TO CROSS-RAILS

1 **Set out the** pales on the ground, using a straight length of lumber to align them at the base. Lay the cross-rails at the desired heights and position the first pale at a distance from the ends of the cross-rails to allow for the width of 1 pale plus half the width of the wooden support post.

2 **Check the angles** with a set square. Attach the pale to the cross-rails, driving 2 nails diagonally into each rail.

3 **Position the next pale,** using the spacer to determine the correct distance from the first. Attach to the cross-rails as before, with 2 nails top and bottom. Continue to the end, checking that each pale is vertical.

4 **Drill 2 guide holes** at each end of both rails. Screw the rails to the support posts. Shape the tops of the support posts as desired, or use shaped post caps.

Installing Posts and Fence Panel

1 **Cut the wooden** posts to length, allowing for the depth of the post-support socket in which the post will sit and the fence's ultimate height above ground level. Lay the panel on the ground in its final position. Place the posts alongside to work out the position for the spiked metal post supports.

2 **Using a post-driving** tool, drive the metal supports into the ground. Insert the posts and check the level on a straightedge laid across them.

3 **Screw the cross-rails** to the wooden posts, using 2 screws at each end of both top and bottom rails.

4 **Protect the fence** by painting or staining in your chosen color and finish. The one used here is a colored wood stain that preserves the wood and adds a vibrant color while allowing the grain of the wood to show through.

BUILDING WALLS

A BRICK WALL MAKES THE PERFECT BOUNDARY for an area, high walls offering the best possible value in security, privacy, and ornament. If a wall is to be strong and safe, it is vital to make an accurate assessment of your skills before you begin: a simple, low brick wall is a realistic achievement for the competent amateur, but higher, more complex walls are best left to the professionals.

MAKING A FOOTING

The higher a wall, the more substantial its foundations must be. For walls up to 3ft (1m) in height, footings should be two to three times the width of the wall with a depth at least equal to the width of the wall (*see table on p.66*). On clay soils or in areas with severe winters, where footings must be below the frost line, it's best to seek expert advice before building. The footing surface must be level, the sides of the trench vertical, and its corners true.

YOU NEED:

TOOLS
- String and pegs
- Measuring tape
- Set square
- Spade
- Straightedge
- Level

MATERIALS
- Crushed stone to fill trench to a depth of 6in (15cm)
- Concrete: 1 part cement to 1½ parts sharp sand to 3½ parts aggregate; or 5 parts combined aggregate to 1 part cement, omitting the sand (as on p.48)

STRIP FOUNDATIONS FOR WALLS

1 **Set out** the position of the required foundations with string and pegs. Using a builder's set square, check that all corners are square and true (*see p.66*).

2 **Dig a trench** of the necessary depth (*see above*). Drive in pegs to the level for the concrete, checking their alignment with a straightedge and level.

3 **Soak the trench** with water and let it drain. Pack in a 6in-(15cm-) layer of crushed stone. Pour in the concrete, slicing with a spade to dispel air bubbles.

4 **Tamp down** the concrete with a length of wood and level it to the top of the pegs. Allow to cure for at least 2 days before starting to build.

◄ A LOW BRICK WALL *A perfect site divider here lends elevation to a display of summer bedding.*

BUILDING A LOW BRICK WALL

For strength and stability, a simple, full-brick wall should be no higher than 3ft (1m). Construction at this height is a realistic do-it-yourself job. Higher walls demand a considerable level of skill and experience. To ensure a uniform finish, use a story pole as a gauge, marked off at 3in (75mm) intervals (for standard bricks with ½in- (10mm-) mortar joints). For the best results, practice throwing mortar and buttering bricks before you begin.

YOU NEED:

TOOLS
- Builder's lines
- Level
- Builder's trowel
- Story pole
- Pointing tool
- Bolster chisel
- Club hammer

MATERIALS
- Standard bricks: allow 50 bricks per square yard (60 per square meter)
- Mortar: 1 part cement to 3 parts soft sand; or 112lb (50kg) premixed mortar per square yard (square meter)

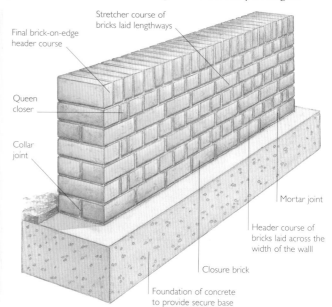

Stretcher course of bricks laid lengthways

Final brick-on-edge header course

Queen closer

Collar joint

Mortar joint

Header course of bricks laid across the width of the walll

Closure brick

Foundation of concrete to provide secure base

SETTING OUT A DRY RUN

1 **Set out the** position of the wall with 2 builder's lines a brick's width plus ½in (10mm) apart. Ensure that the lines are equidistant along the length of the proposed wall.

2 **Lay a dry run** of bricks to check for fit, allowing a ½in- (10mm-) space between each. Check the level of the front edge with a level. Chalk the position of the bricks on the foundations.

LAYING THE FIRST STRETCHER COURSE

1 **Throw a mortar** bed ½in (10mm) thick and 1 brick wide, along the length of the first course. Furrow with the trowel tip.

2 **Lay the first** brick lengthwise on the mortar bed. Check that the brick is level both from end to end and front to back.

3 **Make adjustments** to the level by tapping down gently with the trowel handle. Recheck and do not proceed until it is level.

4 **Set up a builder's line** as a guide to the position for the first course of bricks. Wind the line around a brick at each end to ensure that it remains taut as you work.

5 **Butter the end** face of the next brick, tapering the mortar edges with the trowel to form a ⅝in- (13mm-) thick layer at the center. This will give a ½in- (10mm-) joint.

6 **Working inward** from either end of the wall, set each brick in its marked position, checking levels as you go. To close the course, butter both end faces of the final brick.

7 **Complete the first course** by laying a row of bricks parallel to the first, checking levels along and across. Fill the collar joint between the rows with mortar.

COMPLETING THE WALL

1 **Throw a mortar bed** on top of the first (stretcher) brick course and lay the next brick course (the header) crossways. Check and adjust the levels as before.

2 **Check the height** of each course with a story pole and check constantly for levels. To avoid weak joints, if you make a mistake, remove brick and mortar and start again.

3 **Raise up both ends** of the wall by four courses, alternating stretchers and headers. Scrape off excess mortar with the trowel edge as you bed each brick. Neaten joints with a pointing tool.

4 **Once both ends** have been built up, check the levels from end to end, across the wall, and vertically. Check the height of each course with the story pole.

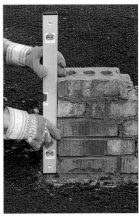

5 **Peg a builder's line** into the mortar joint in the built-up end bricks as a guide for the second course. Make sure that it remains taut.

6 **Insert a queen closer** (*see p.59*) after the first header to maintain staggered joints and avoid having a weak joint running down the wall.

7 **As you build**, constantly check all levels, horizontal and vertical, and the depth of each course. Move the builder's line up for each new course.

8 **Complete the wall** with a header course: throw a mortar bed along the length of the wall. Lay the first brick on edge, crosswise across the wall. Butter one face of each remaining brick and butt it up against the one before. Continue across the length of the wall.

FINISHING THE WALL
To finish the wall and help deflect rainwater, point the mortar joints by running a pointing tool first against the vertical joints, then along the horizontal joints (see also p.69).

CORNERS AND BONDS

Bonding patterns can be both decorative and functional, but not all are equal in structural strength. The stretcher bond is the one most often used for walls that are one brick thick. The English and Flemish bonds are stronger because the header course forms a firm "tie" between the front and back of the wall. Bricks cut in half lengthwise (*see p.59*) are used in alternate courses to ensure that joints are staggered. The diagrams below illustrate the laying pattern used for turning corners.

STRETCHER BOND

Staggered stretchers overlap, with the end of one brick at the center of the one below. Corners are made by alternating stretchers and headers, while half-bats form the final bond at the end of a straight wall.

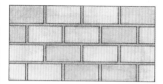

ENGLISH BOND

In this strong bond for two-brick thick walls, alternate courses of stretchers and headers are laid, with a "queen closer" (a brick cut in half along its length) inserted in header courses to stagger joints.

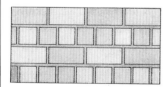

FLEMISH BOND

An alternative to English bond in a two-brick-thick wall, every course in Flemish bond alternates headers and stretchers. Again, joints are staggered by inserting queen closers after the first header.

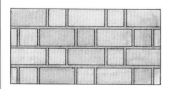

Half-bat forms final bond

Queen closer

Queen closer

A BRICK RETAINING WALL

To create low terraces or a raised bed, retaining walls up to 26in (65cm) high can be constructed simply with a single course in stretcher-bond pattern. Large volumes of soil and water exert great pressures, and, for anything higher than 26in (65cm), it may be necessary to incorporate reinforcing rods. In this case, seek professional advice.

HINTS & TIPS

• In some places, permission is needed for walls higher than 3ft (1m), and regulations may demand professional construction.
• For extra strength, use concrete blocks and face with bricks for an attractive finish.
• A drystone wall (*see p.57*) on a firm foundation can be used for low terraces and forms the ideal niche for many rock plants.

LOW TERRACING
A series of low terraces is a practical self-build proposition and is the ideal way of making a sloping site more accessible. Here, it displays colorful spring bedding plants to perfection.

HOW IT WORKS

A half-brick wall in stretcher bond is built on a concrete footing. A drain (not shown) runs horizontally behind and along the base of the wall, while unmortared vertical joints at every third brick in the lowest course form weep holes; both direct excess water away from the wall. The infill of stone or gravel assists drainage and helps spread the load. The coping stone deflects rainwater from the wall surface.

A mowing strip, just below soil level, makes a neat edge to the lawn and allows it to be mowed cleanly; it is made from quarter-bats (*see Cutting Bricks, p.59*) laid on mortar.

Coping

Gravel infill

Mowing strip of quarter-bats

Weep hole

Concrete footing

Half-bat completes course

DRYSTONE WALLS

A TRUE DRYSTONE WALL (*see p.57*) is built without mortar and relies on the forces of gravity for its strength and integrity. When the stone used reflects local geology, such walls are unsurpassed for natural effects, especially when planted with rock plants such as sedums or sempervivums. Construction is a satisfying task that demands skill and time; the relatively high cost is merely an accurate reflection of the longevity and durability of the finished article.

MAKING A STONE-EFFECT BLOCK WALL

Some manufacturers offer "drystone walling" in kit form. Consistent block size and the use of exterior-grade brick adhesive makes the construction of a realistic facsimile of a drystone wall quick and straightforward. The technique does not allow for integral planting pockets, but, over time, weathering and colonization by lichens, mosses, and self-seeding wall flora such as stonecrops (*Sedum*) will enhance the naturalistic effect.

YOU NEED:

TOOLS
• Spade
• Level
• Notched adhesive spreader

MATERIALS
• Crushed stone and concrete for footings
• Wailing blocks: use standard- (15in/380mm) and two-thirds- (10in/255mm) length blocks for staggered joints
• Quoin-end blocks (i.e. with two adjacent molded faces): (standard- (15in/380mm) and two-thirds- (10in/255mm) length blocks
• Coping blocks: (15in/380mm) length
• Exterior-grade brick adhesive

LAYING FOOTINGS AND FIRST BLOCK

1 Construct footings (*see p.47*) 3 times the width of the wall and 12in (300mm) deep: 8in- (200mm-) stone layer topped with 4in- (100mm-) concrete layer. Allow the concrete to cure for at least 2 days.

2 Apply brick adhesive with a notched adhesive spreader to the lower surface of a two-thirds-length quoin-end block.

3 Place the block at one end of the foundations, aligned with the proposed line of the wall. Check the block for levels.

◀NATURAL HABITAT *Crevices between the stones provide ideal spaces for plants such as sedum.*

BUILDING THE WALL

1 With the first block in place, apply adhesive to a standard-length block. Butt up to the end block; check that the front edges are aligned.

2 Complete the first course, using standard and two-thirds blocks to achieve staggered joints and pressing the blocks firmly together.

3 Start the second course with a standard-length quoin-end block. Check the vertical and horizontal levels as you continue laying blocks.

ADDING THE FINISHING TOUCHES

2 Continue adding coping blocks to the top of the wall, checking alignment as you do so. When the wall is complete, backfill up to the base of the wall with topsoil removed from the footings trench.

1 With the plastic spreader, apply a layer of adhesive to a coping block. Position on top of the finished wall, checking that all outer surfaces are aligned.

THE FINISHED WALL
The wall's pristine appearance will be softened by natural weathering and can be further enhanced by planting self-clinging climbers in the topsoil at the wall's base.

BUILDING A DRYSTONE WALL

Newly quarried stone is expensive, but stone may be obtained more cheaply as unused quarry waste or reclaimed from derelict walls. For the latter you must obtain permission and check local regulations, as removal of stones may be illegal in some areas. For a 3ft- (1m-) high wall, you will need about 1 ton (1 tonne) of stone per linear yard (linear meter). Before you begin, you might like to practice your skills on a drystone-walling course.

ANATOMY OF A DRYSTONE WALL

Foundation stones are set in a level trench, just below ground level. Every stone touches its neighbor, and all joints overlap. Stones are laid level, with the long axis running into the wall, and wedged in with small stones. The gap between the two faces is closely packed as the wall is built. One throughstone per linear yard (linear meter) is inserted halfway up the wall. Copestones are laid from either end toward a central closure and are wedged in place with V-shaped stones.

SORTING STONES INTO TYPES
Before construction begins, stones are sorted into five basic categories according to their position and function within the wall.

Small filling stones pack the space between the two faces

Copestones are wedged in place by hammered-in slices of stone

Throughstones tie faces together at 3ft- (1m-) intervals or less

Building stones decrease in size to give a slope of about 1 in 12

Foundation stones are large, flat, and heavy

PLANTING IN A DRYSTONE WALL

1 **Fill crevice** with soil. Place a small rooted cutting (here, sempervivum) on the flat surface of a stone, easing the roots gently into the crevice.

2 **Pack more soil** into the crevice to hold the plant securely in position. Firm the plant in with your fingertips, adding more soil if necessary.

3 **Once all the plants** are in place (here, saxifrages and sempervivum), water from the top of the wall or with a mist spray. Refirm as needed and keep moist until established.

GETTING DOWN TO BASICS

CHOOSING MATERIALS

THE WEALTH OF WALLING AND FENCING materials available can make selection a confusing task, and choice is full of pitfalls for the unwary. Builder's suppliers and do-it-yourself stores are a prime source of expert advice, but, before approaching them, familiarize yourself with commonly available materials and the terms used to describe them, and be clear about what you hope to achieve.

MATERIALS FOR WALLS

Apart from cost and appearance, the most important factors when choosing materials for outdoor use are durability and frost resistance. Clay bricks are graded for "hardiness": for outdoor use they must be frost- and moisture-resistant if they are not to flake or break in response to freeze–thaw cycles. Do not be tempted to use cheaper, less durable types, and be sure to check the grade if you wish to use recycled bricks.

FROGGED & CORED BRICKS
Filled with mortar, the frog or core helps key in the bricks.

DRYSTONE-EFFECT BLOCKS
Cast in concrete, these blocks are durable and inexpensive.

ROCK-FACED CONCRETE
Finished to look like red bricks or sandstone blocks.

DRESSED STONE BLOCKS
Natural, very expensive, but durable and long lived.

PIERCED CONCRETE BLOCK
Cheap, easy to build, but not structurally strong.

FACING OR STOCK BRICKS
Available in a variety of colors and textures.

CUTTING BRICKS

To cut bricks to size, use a pencil and straightedge to mark a cutting line. Place the brick on a soft surface (here, soft sand). Align bolster chisel with pencil line and strike firmly with a club hammer. Repeat on the opposite face. Place the brick flat and strike again on the pencil line. Repeat each step in turn until the brick breaks.

QUEEN CLOSER AND BATS
Here, a brick is being cut in half lengthwise to produce a "queen closer," which is used in a brick wall to maintain staggered joints. A brick cut across its width is known as a "bat."

CONCRETE OR MORTAR?

Mortar and concrete serve different purposes: concrete is used for footings and foundations, while mortar is used to bond brick, stone, or concrete blocks. Both mortar and concrete use cement as the bonding agent.

For concrete footings and foundations, mix 1 part cement, 2½ parts sharp sand, and 3½ parts ½–¾in (10–20mm) aggregate. For masonry mortar, mix 1 part masonry cement with 3 parts soft sand.

Be sure to use the right sand and cement. Soft, or builder's, sand is fine grade and salt free; sharp sand is coarser. Masonry cement is a ready-made mix with additives designed to lend greater workability.

USEFUL TERMS

Cement: a gray powder containing limestone, that reacts chemically to form a bonding agent when mixed with water.
Concrete: a mix of cement, sharp sand, coarse aggregate, and water.
Mortar: a mix of cement, sand, and water.

MIXING MASONRY MORTAR

1 **Place measured** quantities of dry, soft sand and cement on a suitable flat surface. Mix together thoroughly with a shovel.

2 **Make a well** in the pile of sand and cement and add a little clean water. Blend it in with a shovel, adding more water as necessary.

3 **Mix until smooth** and firm, and furrows made with a shovel hold their shape. If too wet, mortar will run; if too dry, joints will be weak.

DIFFERENT TYPES OF FENCING

The choice of fence is dictated first by its intended function and then by esthetics. If security and privacy are priorities, choose closeboard, panel, or interference fencing. Picket fences make a good-looking boundary but offer little security and no privacy. Ranch-style (planed boards attached horizontally to sturdy posts) and post-and-rail fencing (horizontal poles or rough-sawn lumber between posts) are similarly insecure but form a low-cost boundary. Snow fence is, at best, a temporary measure, while post-and-wire variants play a valuable stockproofing role. Both are best camouflaged by plantings.

LIFE EXPECTANCY

• Lumber that has been pressure treated with preservative is best for outdoor use. If cut on site, be sure to treat all cut surfaces.

• Lumber varies in durability. Oak and white and red cedar have a life of 10–25 years if untreated; some pine, spruce, and Douglas fir last 5–10 years if untreated, extending to 10–25 years with preservative treatment.

• Chainlink or welded galvanized wire last 10 years, more if the wire is plastic coated.

• Very expensive tropical hardwoods, like iroko, last a lifetime, but check that they come from sustainable forestry sources.

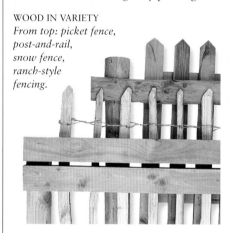

WOOD IN VARIETY
From top: picket fence, post-and-rail, snow fence, ranch-style fencing.

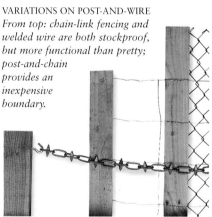

VARIATIONS ON POST-AND-WIRE
From top: chain-link fencing and welded wire are both stockproof, but more functional than pretty; post-and-chain provides an inexpensive boundary.

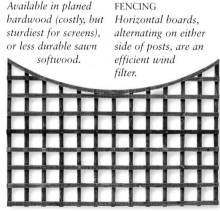

▼TRELLIS
Available in planed hardwood (costly, but sturdiest for screens), or less durable sawn softwood.

►INTERFERENCE FENCING
Horizontal boards, alternating on either side of posts, are an efficient wind filter.

Supporting Posts

A fence is only as strong as its supporting posts; for strength and durability, concrete wins hands down. Concrete outlasts any wood and is maintenance free, even below ground, because it resists the destructive action of ground water. Grooved concrete posts offer an easy slot for panel fences, but, if a less utilitarian appearance is desired, you can use concrete spurs (*right*), which are predrilled for easy fitting of wooden posts.

Pressure-treated wooden posts come twice-weathered (shaped to a point) or flat, to take a decorative weather cap. Pressure-treated rustic poles are available for post-and-rail or rustic-work fences. Even treated lumber rots eventually in contact with wet soil; although an additional coat of preservative prolongs their life, wooden posts that touch damp soil will still need to be replaced within 10–15 years.

FENCE POSTS
A range of fence posts, of varying durability and cost, is available. When considering price, take into account the time and expense of subsequent maintenance treatments.

Grooved concrete post

Tall concrete spur

Wooden post

Treated rustic pole

Choosing Lumber

Although both desirable and suitable for outdoor use, some hardwoods, such as oak, are very expensive. Softwoods, like fir and western red cedar, are less costly. All three are long lived without preservative. Most other softwoods are even less expensive but must be preservative treated. Pressure treatment forces preservative deep into the wood and gives a much longer life than a simple surface coating.

Lumber for outdoor use is often described as durable, as distinct from nondurable woods for indoor use. Lumber merchants offer lumber rough sawn or planed and will often cut to length. Sawn lumber is usually cheapest and fine for most fencing, but choose planed lumber if you wish to apply a wood paint to the finished fence.

PLANED-ALL-AROUND LUMBER
Planed boards have a smooth surface that is ideal for a crisply painted finish.

ROUGH-SAWN LUMBER
This is adequate for most fencing purposes and can be stained to color the wood.

SURFACE-TREATED LUMBER
A surface treatment of preservative is effective but needs to be reapplied regularly.

TOOLS FOR THE JOB

WHATEVER THE TASK AT HAND, it is invariably made easier by using the correct tools for the job. Simple items, such as a straightedge, leveling pegs, or story pole (*see p.50*), can be made at home from scraps of wood. Many small tools, such as pointing trowels, are unlikely to be used frequently, so quality and durability are less important to you than to a professional; in these cases, you can keep outlay down by choosing from the cheaper tools offered.

INVESTING IN TOOLS

For some jobs, high-quality tools really do contribute to achieving a professional finish. For building work, in particular, accurate measurement and leveling are the key to producing safe structures, so buying the best tools that you can afford is easily justified. Good measuring tools will come in handy for many other projects around the home and garden, and, if you keep them clean and take good care of them, they will last a lifetime.

Builder's square

LEVEL AND SQUARE
Clockwise from top left are builder's square, tape, pegs, straightedge, level.

TOOLS FOR WALLS

Brick and stonework need several specialized tools: those shown below are the minimum you need to own, buy, or borrow.

The sturdiest (and most expensive) trowels are cast from a single piece of steel. Those with welded handles often break with prolonged use but are much cheaper and perfectly adequate for one-time jobs.

You may also need a line level, and a soft, long-bristled brush is handy for cleaning surfaces before applying mortar.

CARE OF TOOLS

• Immediately after use, wash in clean water all tools that come into contact with cement or mortar. Both set hard and are difficult to remove if left to dry.

• Keep metal parts sound and rust free by washing, drying, and wiping with an oily rag after use. Store tools in a dry, airy place.

• Wooden handles last longer if wiped over occasionally with linseed oil.

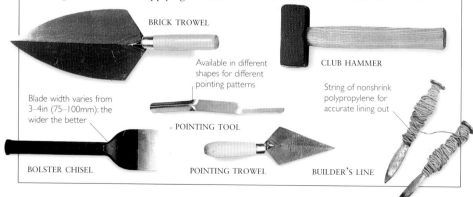

BRICK TROWEL

Available in different shapes for different pointing patterns

CLUB HAMMER

Blade width varies from 3–4in (75–100mm): the wider the better

String of nonshrink polypropylene for accurate lining out

POINTING TOOL

BOLSTER CHISEL

POINTING TROWEL

BUILDER'S LINE

TOOLS FOR FENCES

You may find that most tools needed for fence construction are already part of your home toolkit, but, if you do need to buy, the following are most useful.

A crosscut saw is designed to cut lumber across the grain (ripsaws cut along the grain, and a general purpose saw does both). The easiest way to cut fancy shapes is with a jigsaw attachment on a power drill; if you need to do it by hand, use a fret saw or coping saw.

A chisel and wooden-headed mallet are used for cutting slot or mortise joints. Mortise chisels have handles that are reinforced to take punishment from the mallet; a bevel-edge chisel is similar but, being slightly broader, is easier and quicker for the amateur to use.

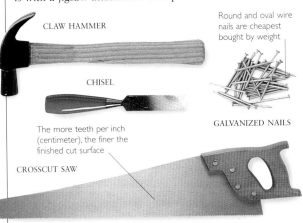

CLAW HAMMER

Round and oval wire nails are cheapest bought by weight

CHISEL

GALVANIZED NAILS

The more teeth per inch (centimeter), the finer the finished cut surface

CROSSCUT SAW

SAFE USE OF POWER TOOLS

- Always be sure to use properly grounded equipment when using power tools outdoors.
- Never use electrical tools during or just after rain.
- Use grounded extension cords with the same number of wires as the tool.
- Disconnect power before adjusting, inspecting, or cleaning an electrical tool.

RENTING SPECIALIZED EQUIPMENT

Good specialized rental companies carry an extensive range of tools and machinery, so it is always worth checking what is offered before buying tools that you may use only once. They will also advise on the most suitable equipment for the job at hand. Renting can be for a full or half day.

Digging post holes and mixing concrete or mortar, in particular, require strength and fitness. A manual post-hole borer or auger is helpful for extensive runs of fencing, and a concrete mixer saves a good deal of effort when laying footings.

It is essential, especially if you are not used to operating machinery, that you get a demonstration of how equipment works and how to use it safely. Before accepting delivery of any rented items, check that everything looks well maintained and that equipment is running smoothly.

CHECKLIST

- Check the condition and smooth running of equipment before accepting delivery.
- Ask for a demonstration and ensure that you know how to operate all machinery safely. Don't forget to check on fuel requirements for motorized machines.
- Make sure that you wear any appropriate safety gear; you may be able to rent goggles and ear protectors.
- When using concrete mixers, wear close-fitting clothing and sturdy gloves and shoes. Keep your head, hands, and shovels clear of moving parts.
- Make all possible preparations, such as lining out and trench digging, before taking delivery of rented equipment.
- Do not underestimate how long you will need the rented equipment: you may be charged a higher rate for additional days.

Preparing for Action

BY THE TIME YOU ARE READY TO BUILD, you will have made sure that your skills are adequate for safe completion of the project and that the project conforms with any legal and building regulation requirements. Accurately work out overall dimensions in readiness for estimating and ordering materials. Plan ahead for taking delivery, giving consideration to site access and storage of materials. If necessary, recruit a team of helpers to move heavy items.

Ordering and Delivery

Calculating quantities is a daunting task for the beginner, but a reputable builder's store or do-it-yourself supplier will be happy to advise if given accurate dimensions for the task at hand.

Ask about the supplier's sale or return policy: many accept returns of unopened bagged materials. Check transportation and delivery arrangements, and be on hand to ensure that delivery is made as near to the site as possible to minimize the heavy labor of transporting materials later.

Have ready wooden pallets and plastic sheeting to provide dry, off-ground storage of bricks and cement.

ESTIMATING QUANTITIES

- When estimating quantities, work in either imperial or metric measurements: do not mix the two.
- Area equals length x width.
- Volume equals length x width x depth.
- For a half-brick wall, you will need 50 bricks per square yard (60 per square meter); 100 (120) for a full-brick wall. You will need 8–10 concrete walling blocks per square yard (10–12 per square meter). Allow 5–10% for waste.
- Calculate concrete and its constituents by volume in cubic yards (cubic meters).

A GLOSSARY OF USEFUL TERMS

Aggregate: crushed stone or gravel (usually ½–¾in- (10–20mm-) grade) used in making concrete.

Bat: a piece of a whole brick. A half-bat is a brick cut in half across its width; a quarter-bat is half the length of a half-bat.

Bed: a horizontal layer of mortar on which bricks are laid.

Bond: the arrangement of bricks in a wall (bond pattern, *see p.52*), or the area of adhesion between masonry units.

Buttering: applying mortar to a brick face.

Closer: the final brick that closes a course. A brick cut in half along its length is sometimes called a queen closer.

Coping: protective cap, often made of precast concrete, laid on top of a wall to shed water.

Course: a layer of bricks in a structure. Bricks in the **header** course lie across the wall; **stretchers** line up along the length of wall.

Crushed stone: material used as a subbase for concrete footings.

Face: the exposed surface of a brick.

Footing: the concrete layer of a foundation.

Foundation: the below-ground structural support for a structure.

Header: *see* **Course**

Joint: the layer of mortar between bricks, usually a standard ½in (10mm). Cross joints are vertical joints; bed joints are horizontal. Collar joints link two sides of a wall together.

Lead: 3–4 courses of bricks built up at the ends of a wall before building the body of the wall.

Pointing: the surface finish of a mortar joint.

Stretcher: *see* **Course**

Throwing: the act of applying mortar to a bed.

Twice-weathered: (of lumber or concrete copings) shaped to a point with two sides.

Weep hole: a vertical, unmortarted gap between two bricks to allow for drainage.

BUILDING AND PLANNING REGULATIONS

Much building and planning legislation is framed primarily with public safety in mind. For example, the height restrictions on walls and fences are designed to prevent the obstruction of clear visibility on public highways. The panel below contains an outline of the law as applied to walls and fences – but it must be emphasized, if you have any doubts at all, for the safety of yourself and others, seek expert advice.

PLANNING REGULATIONS ON WALLS AND FENCES

• If a wall or fence lies on a boundary between two properties, or fronts onto a highway or public thoroughfare, it must lie on your side of the boundary. It is always prudent and polite to consult your neighbors before constructing walls or fences.

• The height and other aspects of a gate, wall, or fence are often regulated by state and local building codes and ordinances. For example, constructing a fence 6ft (2m) tall or higher may require you to submit a detailed plan to your local planning agency showing exactly what and where you intend to build. Other ordinances may require any contractors you may employ to be registered with the state and/or local boards. You and your contractor may need to pay fees.

• Consultation: if you are at all unsure about your project, it is advisable to consult your local government's building or planning agency to check whether planning permission is needed for a wall or fence. The building and planning control officers of your municipality are the experts; seek their help rather than after the event. Remember that they are empowered to make you remove structures that contravene the law.

PRECAUTIONS AND SAFETY

Garden and do-it-yourself accidents account for a major proportion of home-based incidents, and the potential for serious injury increases when using heavy machinery and electrical tools. Ensure that powered equipment is in good order and that you know how to use it. Wear sturdy gloves to keep mortar and cement off your skin; in the event of contact, wash in copious amounts of clean water to avoid burns. Protect your eyes with goggles whenever you cut brick or stone.

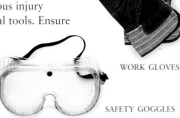

WORK GLOVES

SAFETY GOGGLES

INCORRECT POSTURE

CORRECT POSTURE

PROTECT YOUR BACK
Never lift by bending from the waist: use the strength of your legs – not your lumbar region – to lift the load. Don't attempt to twist and lift at the same time: you can injure your back by reaching and lifting even relatively light weights. Always carry heavy weights close to your body, and use a barrow or dolly whenever possible. Don't overestimate your strength.

LEVEL AND TRUE

The safety and stability of any structure depends on all corners being square, all lines being straight, and every surface being level in three directions: along its length, across its width, and vertically. Check these three levels constantly during construction.

To find a true corner, mark the line of a wall with two pegs, one at either end. Measure 16in (40cm) along the line beyond the desired position of the corner. Place a second peg, by eye, at right angles to the line, 12in (30cm) away from the corner, and then adjust its position until the diagonal line between the two pegs measures 20in (50cm). The corner opposite the 20in (50cm) side of a triangle so constructed is a perfect right angle, as are all four angles around the corner point (*see illustration right*).

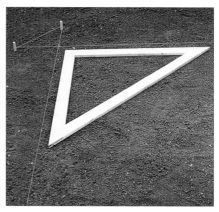

MARKING OUT A TRUE CORNER
Use simple geometry to create a corner: all triangles with sides in the proportions 3:4:5 form a right-angled corner opposite the longest side. Check with a builder's square.

THE IMPORTANCE OF FOUNDATIONS

A wall is only as strong as its foundations, whose dimensions are calculated according to the size of the wall, the method of construction, and soil type and condition.

Most walls up to 26in (65cm) high do not need substantial foundations. Those 26–39in (65–100cm) in height need a concrete foundation two to three times the width of the wall, with a depth at least equal to the wall's width. The footing must have a level surface, with straight and true sides. Since its base must be on firm subsoil, the depth

may need to be increased. In areas with severe winters, footings must be deeper so that they are below the frost line.

Half-brick walls should be no higher than 26in (65cm), and, if higher than 18in (45cm), they must have supporting piers at 10ft- (3m-) intervals. Full-brick walls higher than 26in (65cm) must be built with a bond that ties the wall together.

For walls over 3ft (1m) in height, especially those on clay or silt soils, it is advisable to seek professional advice.

GUIDELINE DIMENSIONS FOR SELF-BUILT WALLS

TYPE OF WALL	WALL HEIGHT	FOOTING DEPTH	FOOTING WIDTH
• **Half-brick wall** 4in (102mm) thick	• 18–26in (45–65cm)	• 4½–6in (110–150mm)	• 8–12in (205–300mm)
• **Piers** for half-brick wall	• 18–26in (45–65cm)	• 18–24in (460–610mm)	• 18–24in (460–610mm)
• **Full-brick wall** 8in (215mm) thick	• Up to 3ft (1m)	• 9–12in (230–300mm)	• 18–24in (450–600mm)

LOOKING AFTER YOUR STRUCTURES

All structures, whether of wood, brick, or stone, need a degree of maintenance to protect the investment of time, effort, and money that they represent. For brick and stonework, only low-level, infrequent maintenance is required, but wood is more demanding. Pressure-treated and naturally durable wood, like oak and cedar, need only occasional applications of additional preservatives, while less durable and untreated wood requires more regular treatment.

PRESERVING WOOD

Preservatives come in several forms and in a range of colors: apply creosote and water-based types every four years, those based on solvent every two to three years. Creosote is toxic to plants and poisonous if swallowed, inhaled, or absorbed via the skin, so solvent-based types are usually preferable. Since the range is confusingly wide, check with the supplier that the one you have chosen fits the particular job.

GO WITH THE GRAIN
Always apply wood treatments to clean, dry, dust-free surfaces, and paint along the grain of the wood. First test the color on a small area to check the effect.

THE RIGHT FINISH

There are two basic methods of coloring wood: with paint or with stain. Wood stains darken and/or color the wood, but, being translucent, they still allow the beauty of the grain to show through. Many exterior-grade wood stains also include preservative; they are prepared in a water, solvent, or oil base. In general, the latter are the easiest to apply: they dry slowly.

Exterior wood paints are acrylics, specially formulated to give a finish that allows the wood to "breathe," thus reducing flaking and cracking. For a long-lasting finish, apply over coats of wood primer and undercoat. To achieve a smooth finish on planed lumber, rub off rough spots and edges with sandpaper, then wipe with turpentine to remove any dust.

HINTS AND TIPS

• Make sure that all freshly cut lumber surfaces are treated with preservative, even when using pressure-treated lumber.
• Keep all preservatives, especially creosote, away from plants and off your skin by wearing protective gloves and clothing.
• Apply paints, stains, and preservatives to dry, clean, dust-free lumber. Always work along the grain with a good-quality brush that will not shed its bristles as you work.
• Use only exterior-grade wood paints outdoors, and don't forget the end grain. Using a primer and undercoat made by the same manufacturer guarantees compatibility.
• For all surface finishes, always read the label advice with regard to number of coats needed, drying time, and coverage.

REPLACING ROTTEN POSTS

Concrete spurs have a clear advantage when it comes to post replacement; simply unbolt the old post and bolt the new one in place. You may be able to lift and replace posts set in concrete if the footing is sound, filling any gaps with instant cement to avoid water penetration. If not, you will need to dig out and renew both post and foundation.

REMOVING A ROTTEN POST
Lash a scrap of wood to the bottom of the rotten post as near to the ground as possible. Using a large stone as a pivot, apply downward pressure to lever out the the post.

Damaged post

Stone

Wood scrap

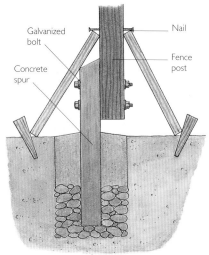

Galvanized bolt

Nail

Concrete spur

Fence post

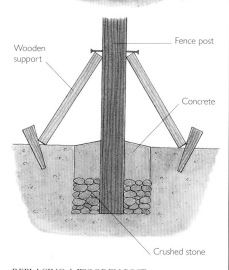

Wooden support

Fence post

Concrete

Crushed stone

REPLACING A POST ON A CONCRETE SPUR
Drive two nails into the damaged post and take the weight of the post by bracing, as shown, before unbolting. Mark and predrill bolt holes in the new post before replacing.

REPLACING A WOODEN POST
Detach panels; dig out post and foundations. Renew post and foundation (see p.31–32). Brace the new post vertically and leave in place for a week until the concrete has cured.

WIRE PLANT SUPPORTS FOR FENCES

Attach horizontal or vertical wires to vine eyes screwed into the support posts. To avoid sagging, tauten the wires by tightening the vine eyes with pliers or by using tensioners. Space wires 12–18in (30–45cm) apart, with the lowest 12in (30cm) above soil level.

Vine eye

USING VINE EYES
Allow a minimum 2in (5cm) clearance between fence and wire to permit adequate air circulation and reduce the risk of fungal diseases.

REPOINTING BRICKWORK

Well-built walls may not need attention for 10–15 years, but any repointing should be done as soon as it is necessary. Remove old mortar with a cold chisel and club hammer to a depth of ¾in (2cm). Mist joints with a fine water spray and repoint. Cover with a plastic sheet for about four days to ensure the slow cure needed for strong joints.

PROS AND CONS

• V-shaped birdsmouth, recessed weather-struck, or half-round patterns shed water well and are the most durable for outdoor use.
• Rubbed and flush pointings shed water moderately well and are acceptably durable outdoors if used with a concrete coping.

| BIRDSMOUTH | WEATHER-STRUCK | HALF-ROUND | RUBBED | FLUSH |

PAINTING WALLS

A stucco-rendered surface (coated in a mix of one part cement to three to five parts fine sand) gives the finest surface for painting, but even regular brickwork can be given a coat of color provided you use paints that are formulated for outdoor use.

Prepare surfaces thoroughly so that they are clean and dust free, and deal with any small cracks before painting. Check and follow manufacturer's recommendations for priming requirements, since these vary according to formulation.

PAINTS FOR WALLS

Exterior latex paint is available in a wide range of colors and, although water based, is surprisingly durable for outdoor use. Apply to sound, clean surfaces with a good-quality brush or roller.

Masonry paint is an exceptionally hard-wearing finish for rendered surfaces, since it usually contains silica or nylon additives for strong cohesion. Surfaces usually need priming with stabilizers; fungicides may also be recommended to reduce staining.

ATTACHING A TRELLIS TO A WALL

The simplest method is to screw trellis panels onto a framework of vertical, 2in- (5cm-) thick wooden battens. A hooked and hinged fixing allows access to the wall for maintenance: attach horizontal battens to both wall and trellis panel, with two hinges at the bottom and hooks and vine eyes on both sides at the top.

BATTEN
Using galvanized screws, fit vertical battens, at least 2in (5cm) thick, to the wall.

BOTTOM-HINGED
Two sturdy hinges attached to horizontal battens allow a trellis panel to be lowered.

TOP HOOKS
A hook and vine eye on both sides of the batten hold the trellis panel in place.

INDEX

ACKNOWLEDGMENTS

Picture research Cathie Arrington
Special photography Peter Anderson and Steve Gorton
Illustrations Vanessa Luff
Additional illustrations Karen Gavin
Index Hilary Bird

Dorling Kindersley would like to thank:
Marshalls for generously providing advice and materials for the stone-effect block wall; John Murphy for his bricklaying skills; Candida Frith-Macdonald and Anna Hayman for editorial assistance; and all staff at the RHS, in particular Susanne Mitchell, Karen Wilson and Barbara Haynes at Vincent Square, and Nick Freed at Wisley.

American Horticultural Society
Visit AHS at www.ahs.org or call them at 1-800-777-7931 ext. 10. Membership benefits include *The American Gardener* magazine, free admission to flower shows, the free seed exchange, book services, and the Gardener's Information Service.

Photography
The publisher would also like to thank the following for their kind permission to reproduce their photographs:

(key: t=top, c=centre, b=below, l=left, r=right, fc=front cover, bc=back cover)

Garden Picture Library: John Baker 8; Mark Bolton 23t; Rex Butcher 16t, Brian Carter 19t, 53c; Vaughan Fleming 19bl; Jacqui Hurst 15b; Ann Kelly 22t; Lamontagne 17b; Jerry Pavia 9t, 13tl, 13b; Gary Rogers 4bl, 41b; J.S. Sira 46; Janet Sorrell 2, 20b; Ron Sutherland 5bl, 7, 11r, 14b, 16b, 17tl; Nigel Temple 54; Brigitte Thomas 13tr, 14t, 26l; Mel Watson 18
John Glover Photography: 20t, 21
Harpur Garden Library: 42
Clive Nichols Garden Pictures: L. Hampden/J & C Nichols 5br, 10; Leeds City Council – Chelsea 1998 4br, 15t, 22c; Andrew & Karla Newell 23b
Photos Horticultural: 6, 9b, 11l, 12c, 12b, 17tr, 19br, 24, 25, 27, 28r, 29, 30, 36

Cover: commissioned photography with the exception of **Garden Picture Library:** Rex Butcher fc bl; Vaughan Fleming fc tl; Jerry Pavia bc tl; Ron Sutherland bc flap; Mel Watson fc flap; **John Glover:** fc cl; **Clive Nichols Garden Pictures:** Leeds City Council – Chelsea 1998 bc b, bc tr